WOMEN OF AMERICA

Dolley Madison

FIRST LADY OF THE LAND

MATTHEW G. GRANT

Illustrated by Nancy Inderieden

GALLERY OF GREAT AMERICANS SERIES

★ ★

Dolley Madison

FIRST LADY OF THE LAND

Text copyright © 1974 by Publication Associates. Illustrations copyright © 1974 by Creative Education. International copyrights reserved in all countries. No part of this book may be reproduced in any form without written permission from the publisher. Printed in the United States.

Library of Congress Number: 73-15848   ISBN: 0-87191-308-9

Published by Creative Education, Mankato, Minnesota 56001
Distributed by Childrens Press, 1224 West Van Buren Street, Chicago, Illinois 60607

LIBRARY OF CONGRESS CATALOGING IN PUBLICATION DATA
Grant, Matthew G
     Dolley Madison.
     (His Gallery of great American series. Women of America)
     SUMMARY: A biography of the First Lady noted for the graciousness and unprecedented elegance she brought to early nineteenth-century Washington.
     1. Madison, Dolley (Payne) Todd, 1768-1849 — Juvenile literature. [1. Madison, Dolley (Payne) Todd, 1768-1849.   2. Presidents — Wives]
I. Inderieden, Nancy, illus. II. Title.
E342.1.G72   973.5'1'0924 [B] [92]   73-15848
ISBN 0-87191-308-9

DOLLY MADISON'S WORLD

CONTENTS

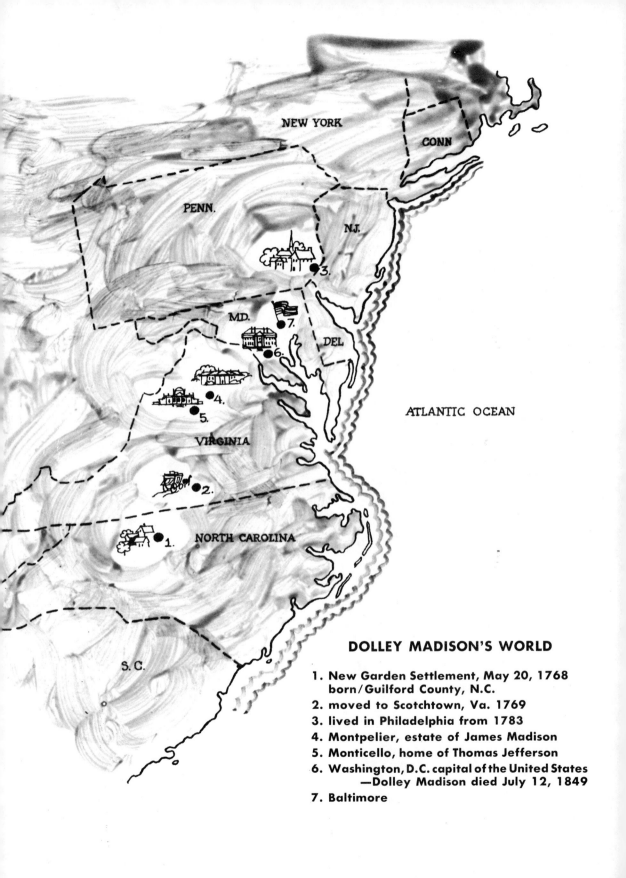

NEW YORK

CONN

PENN.

N.J.

●3.

MD.

●7.

DEL

●6.

ATLANTIC OCEAN

●4.

●5.

VIRGINIA

●2.

●1.

NORTH CAROLINA

S. C.

DOLLEY MADISON'S WORLD

1. New Garden Settlement, May 20, 1768
   born/Guilford County, N.C.
2. moved to Scotchtown, Va. 1769
3. lived in Philadelphia from 1783
4. Montpelier, estate of James Madison
5. Monticello, home of Thomas Jefferson
6. Washington, D.C. capital of the United States
   —Dolley Madison died July 12, 1849
7. Baltimore

THE YOUNG QUAKER

Little Dolley Payne wore gray dresses and plain bonnets. She was not allowed to dance or sing. A simple way of life was part of her Quaker faith. But Dolley was a merry child by nature.

Quakers believed in sending girls to school. So Dolley had an education, unlike the daughters of the rich Virginia planters who lived nearby. She grew up to be clever and witty. And beautiful, too, even though her Quaker parents tried not to notice it.

In 1783, her father freed his slaves and moved to Philadelphia. When Dolley was 22, in 1790, she wed a young Quaker lawyer named John Todd.

The American Revolution had been won. Philadelphia was the capital of the United States. It was the most lively city in the whole country.

Dolley's husband prospered. They moved into a nice home. The marriage was a happy one and two sons were born to the Todds.

Then, in August 1793, a terrible epidemic of yellow fever broke out in Philadelphia.

John Todd rushed his little family out of the city. He himself returned to help care for the sick. It was his duty as a Quaker. By doing this good work he took sick himself. Longing to be with Dolley, he rode to the place where she was staying and died in her arms.

Poor Dolley became very ill herself. Her baby, William, died. After some weeks Dolley recovered and went back to Philadelphia to start life all over.

The fever had disappeared. People streamed back into town—among them officials of the government.

In the spring, Dolley would go walking with her little son, Payne. Her beauty caused men to stare in admiration. Among them was a 43-year-old "confirmed bachelor" named James Madison. He was a small man, only 5 feet 6 inches in height. But his wisdom was gigantic. He had helped frame the constitution.

THE GREAT LITTLE MADISON

Now this important man asked to be presented to the Widow Todd. Dolley was all a-flutter. She wrote a friend: ''Thee must come to me! The great little Madison has asked to see me this evening!''

Madison seems to have fallen in love with Dolley almost at first sight. Not long after their first meeting, he asked her to be his wife. She hesitated. Madison was not a Quaker. If she married him, she would be expelled from the church.

Then Martha Washington sent for Dolley, asking: "Is it true that you are engaged to James Madison?"

Dolley stammered, "No—I think not."

Martha said kindly: "If it is so, be proud of it. He will make thee a good husband, even though he is 17 years older than thee."

Martha told the amazed Dolley that even President Washington hoped she would marry Madison. He had an important government career ahead of him. A wife such as Dolley, full of charm and wit, could be a great help. And besides—he was in love with her!

A STATESMAN'S WIFE

With some doubts lingering, Dolley was married to James Madison September 15, 1794. Before long her admiration for him turned to sincere love. They lived first in Philadelphia and then in Virginia.

The Madison estate, Montpelier, had many visitors. Thomas Jefferson was the Madisons' neighbor. Important men in government

often came to confer. Dolley turned from a
quiet Quaker housewife into an expert hostess.
She put away her plain clothing and wore the
latest styles. Her graciousness made even
quarreling politicians friendly and smiling.
James Madison was very proud of his lovely
new wife.

In 1801, Thomas Jefferson was elected President. He asked Madison to be his Secretary of State.

The Madisons packed up and moved to the brand-new capital city, Washington, D.C. It was still mostly open fields and swamps. The "President's Palace," where Jefferson lived, was a gray, half-empty place. The Madisons were invited to live there. Jefferson was a widower, so Dolley became his hostess.

Later, the Madisons moved into their own house. But Dolley continued her duties as unofficial First Lady. She also gave dances and parties at her own home that were the talk of Washington.

Jefferson was grateful for Dolley's glitter. It helped people forget the troubles of the infant United States. It began to look as

though America and England would go to war.

Jefferson served two terms. Then James Madison was elected President of the United States in 1808, the fourth man to hold the highest office in the land.

Dolley moved into an empty President's Palace. The furniture had belonged to Jefferson. At Dolley's request, Congress set aside money to buy beautiful new furnishings that would remain permanently. Dolley herself supervised the decorating.

As First Lady, she brought an elegance to the U.S. capital. Foreign visitors, who had once scoffed at the "primitive" social life in

Washington, now sat down to splendid meals or attended stately balls that were the equal of those in Europe. Dolley also gave smaller parties and receptions for the common people. She even introduced egg-rolling on the presidential lawn on Easter Monday.

BURNING THE WHITE HOUSE

In 1812, England provoked the United States to war. For the first two years of Madison's second term, the war went badly for the Americans. And in 1814, the British invaded Washington itself.

Madison was away with the army. With the British on their way, Dolley knew she would have to flee. She had servants pack up important papers from the office of the President. She even took down a large portrait of George Washington from the dining room wall.

Then she drove away with her treasures. Not long afterward, the British set the city on fire. The President's Palace was destroyed.

In 1815, the war with the British ended. Washington was rebuilt. The Palace—its stone front newly painted white—was rebuilt and called the White House. The Madisons did not live in it again, however. The President's term ended in 1816, two years before the rebuilding was completed. By then, James and Dolley Madison had retired to the peace of Montpelier.

They lived there for the next 20 years.

James Madison died in 1836. Lonely and sad, Dolley went back to Washington. There she became a social leader once more. People remembered her. Presidents Jackson, Van Buren, Tyler, and Polk were her close friends.

When Dolley Madison died, July 12, 1849, the United States mourned the loss of its most beloved First Lady.

GALLERY OF GREAT AMERICANS SERIES

INDIANS OF AMERICA
GERONIMO
CRAZY HORSE
CHIEF JOSEPH
PONTIAC
SQUANTO
OSCEOLA

EXPLORERS OF AMERICA
COLUMBUS
LEIF ERICSON
DeSOTO
LEWIS AND CLARK
CHAMPLAIN
CORONADO

FRONTIERSMEN OF AMERICA
DANIEL BOONE
BUFFALO BILL
JIM BRIDGER
FRANCIS MARION
DAVY CROCKETT
KIT CARSON

WAR HEROES OF AMERICA
JOHN PAUL JONES
PAUL REVERE
ROBERT E. LEE
ULYSSES S. GRANT
SAM HOUSTON
LAFAYETTE

WOMEN OF AMERICA
CLARA BARTON
JANE ADDAMS
ELIZABETH BLACKWELL
HARRIET TUBMAN
SUSAN B. ANTHONY
DOLLEY MADISON